AROUND THE WORLD SERIES

101 FACTS OF EVERY COUNTRY ON THE PLANET

Part 1: Afghanistan

Ritesh Biswas

101 Facts of Every Country on the Planet | Part 1: Afghanistan

101 Facts of Every Country on the Planet | Part 1: Afghanistan
RITESH BISWAS

Test Edition - 2025
First FL Edition- 2025-26

Cover Credits:
Photo by United Nations Photo licensed under CC BY-NC-ND

Thank you Shantanu Sir for opening up new horizons for me

A Little Note

I randomly came up with the idea of just writing a book. Easy money. The problem was that I was not getting suitable topics to write about.

I pondered and pondered over various topics until I stumbled upon one of my favourite subjects among my diverse portfolio of interests. Geopolitics. I can write stuff on it any day of the week.

But the world of Geopolitics is constantly shifting. What may be relevant today could be hardly worth mentioning the next day. One wrong step and stuff could be a flop.

I then found another topic that would go well. Facts! I'm really a facts guy and thought, "What if I make a book on facts about countries of the world?", and that's how *101 Facts of Every Country on the Planet* was born. Boom! Enough Content to go on to make a reaaaaally long series.

Man.. but finding some way to publish this was an absolute pain as well. For a while I was scrambling to publish this. Then I came across Google Play Books who basically said that this fact book on Afghanistan violates their policy or something (I don't really remember). I am really grateful to the publisher who agreed to publish this, without whose help, this wouldn't have existed.

I took a bit of data from Wikipedia, various Google sites and Geography Now. I apologise for not being specific for such important credits but I messed up my sources. Please forgive me this time.

If you are reading this chances are you bought this and I am deeply grateful to you for doing so in exchange for your time and money. It took a while for me to work on this and hopefully this will be worth your time (and money :))

Without further ado, let's go on to learn about the hidden gems of the world, shall we?

Ritesh Biswas
Author

Afghanistan

Afghanistan, a landlocked country in Central Asia, is known for its rugged mountains and a rich history. It has faced decades of conflict and instability, impacting its political and social development.

[1]

[2]

[3]

[4]

So, What are We Waiting For? Let's Dive into Information!

---

[1] Flag of Afghanistan
[2] Afghanistan on a Map
[3] Hindu Kush Mountains, Afghanistan
[4] Band-e Amir, Afghanistan

Facts About Afghanistan

1. Afghanistan (as of 2024) is officially known as "The Islamic Emirate of Afghanistan" and runs under another flag.

This is the Official Flag of The Islamic Emirate of Afghanistan (as of 2024)

2. Afghanistan has no coastline, making it a landlocked country. Its neighbours are Pakistan, Iran, Turkmenistan, Uzbekistan, Tajikistan and China.
3. Afghanistan's border with China makes it the greatest terrestrial time zone difference on the planet. The difference is 3.5 hours. Afghanistan runs on UTC +04:30 and China runs on UTC +8:00.
   For Example, You are at the Sino-Afghan border on the Afghan side at 8 in the morning and somehow get to the other side in a minute (which isn't actually possible cause.... good luck crossing over the Pamir Mountains) and the time would be 11:31 in just one minute.
4. The country is predominantly mountainous. It has plains in the North and South-east which are separated by the Hindu Kush Mountains, a part of the Himalayas.

5. Some glaciers in the Hindu Kush range are covered with layers of black dust and debris, forming "black ice glaciers." This phenomenon occurs due to high-altitude volcanic dust and environmental deposits. Despite their dark appearance, they are crucial water sources for nearby communities.
6. Afghanistan is home to the endangered snow leopard, with several conservation efforts underway. The country's rugged Hindu Kush mountain range provides a habitat for these elusive big cats, which are well adapted to the harsh, high-altitude environment. Snow leopards in Afghanistan inhabit the central and eastern regions of the country, particularly in the provinces of Badakhshan, Takhar, and Panjshir. They are found in the Hindu Kush mountain range, where they inhabit alpine meadows, rocky outcrops, and scrub forests.
7. The country experiences an arid climate, with hot summers and cold winters that can be extreme across the country.
8. These weather conditions make Afghanistan a suitable place for growing Wheat, Corn and Barley. In Irrigated Areas, Rice and Cotton could also grow. Afghani dry fruits are famous worldwide. Opium Poppy seeds are also grown.
9. Afghanistan produces some of the world's highest-quality saffron, frequently winning international awards for its purity and flavor.

10. Afghanistan is home to ancient pistachio forests, particularly in the north. These forests are both ecologically and economically significant.
11. Afghanistan's economy mainly relies on Agriculture employing around 40–50% of the population. Other key sectors include mining and services, with informal trade and remittances playing a major role.
12. The nation is rich in natural resources like copper, lithium, and iron ore.
13. Since Afghanistan has good land for growing Opium, the crop is grown here. Afghanistan is a big source and medium of opium production and trafficking.
14. Afghanistan has a land area of Approximately 652,864 square kilometers with 12% of the land being arable.
15. *Kabul* is the capital of the country and the largest city. It is located in a valley in the Hindu Kush Mountains and at an elevation of 1790 metres, it is one of the highest capital cities in the world.
16. Kabul is also said to be about one of the oldest cities in the world being about 3500 years old.
17. Kabul's city walls are one of the oldest in the world. These city walls date back to the 6th century.
18. The bazaar of Kabul also known as the "Mandavi Bazaar" has been in operation for over 500 years. The Mandavi is a vibrant and historic bazaar that embodies the spirit of Kabul and Afghanistan. As a cultural and

economic hub, it continues to play a vital role in the lives of locals and visitors alike.

19. The Paghman Gardens, Located near Kabul, are royal gardens modeled after European-style parks in the early 20th century and remain a symbol of pre-war elegance.
20. The official languages of Afghanistan are Pashto and Dari. Dari is a dialect of Persian and it won't be a problem to understand if a Persian talks to a Dari in Persian or a Dari talks to a Persian in Dari. They'll understand each other. Accounting various languages of diverse groups there are about 40 languages spoken throughout Afghanistan.
21. There are Diverse Ethnicities in Afghanistan, such as (From most popular to least) Pashtuns, Tajiks, Hazaras, Uzbeks, Aimaqs, Turkmens, Baloch and other minorities.
22. The Country is predominantly Muslim (over 99%), with Sunni Islam being the majority sect.
23. Their Demonym is (at this point should be well known) *Afghan*.
24. Afghanistan's currency is *Afghan Afghani*.
25. The Wakhan Corridor is a narrow strip of territory in the Badakhshan province of Afghanistan. This corridor stretches eastward, connecting Afghanistan to Xinjiang, China. It also separates the Gorno-Badakhshan Autonomous Region of Tajikistan in the north from the Khyber Pakhtunkhwa and Gilgit-Baltistan regions of

Pakistan in the south, the latter of which is also part of the disputed region of Kashmir.

This high mountain valley, which rises to a maximum altitude of 4,923 m, serves as the source of both the Panj and Pamir rivers, which converge to form the larger Amu Darya River.

For countless centuries, a vital trade route has traversed this valley, facilitating the movement of travelers to and from East, South, and Central Asia.

26. Afghanistan's Wakhan Corridor is home to several pristine alpine lakes that remain virtually untouched by modern development. These lakes, such as Lake Chaqmaqtin, are fed by glaciers and are considered sacred by local Wakhi and Kyrgyz communities. Their remoteness makes them some of the most isolated water bodies in the world.

27. Afghanistan's *Tang-e Gharu* gorge, with its towering cliffs and river-carved valleys, rivals some of the world's most dramatic landscapes. The cliffs of the gorge are a blue-grey limestone, which was formed some 250 million years ago. The Kabul River passes through the gorge, flowing eastward. The Kabul-Jalalabad Road runs through the gorge, parallel to the river.

28. The *Pamir Mountains*, often called the *Roof of the World*, dominate northeastern Afghanistan and extend into Tajikistan, China, and Pakistan.

    The *Panj River*, one of the main rivers in the Pamir

region, forms part of the border between Afghanistan and Tajikistan. It eventually merges with other tributaries to form the *Amu Darya River*, which runs along Afghanistan's northern borders with Tajikistan, Turkmenistan, and Uzbekistan.

The Amu Darya is vital for irrigation, hydroelectric power, and as a natural boundary in an otherwise arid region, supporting agriculture and settlements along its course. Together, the Pamirs and these rivers shape both the geography and the livelihoods of communities in northeastern Afghanistan.

29. *The Helmand river* is the longest river in Afghanistan and the primary watershed for the endorheic Sistan Basin. It originates in the Hindu Kush mountains, where it is separated from the watershed of the Kabul River by the Unai Pass.

30. Along parts of the Helmand River are stretches of black sand, rich in magnetite and other minerals. Locals have used this sand for centuries in traditional medicine and metallurgy. Its dark shimmer contrasts strikingly with the surrounding desert.

31. Near the Helmand River in Lashkar Gah, are the ruins of the ancient *Lashkari Bazaar citadel*, built during the Ghaznavid dynasty (10th–12th centuries).

This sprawling palace complex showcased advanced engineering, with gardens, baths, and frescoes that rivaled the grandeur of other medieval Islamic architecture. Despite its significance, the site remains largely unexplored.

32. The Kabul River is also a long river by Kabul which originates in the Hindu Kush mountains, where it is separated from the watershed of the Helmand River by the Unai Pass.
33. *Band-e Amir* is a series of beautiful turquoise lakes in the central highlands of the nation. It is one of the natural (and national) treasures of Afghanistan, and this is mostly the reason people travel to the country.
34. *The Panjshir valley* in Northeastern Afghanistan has a near-mythical reputation for its geographic ability to resist invasions, thanks to its narrow entry points and steep cliffs. It is impossible to plan invasions by this route.
35. The Panjshir Valley is not only famous for its resistance during conflicts but also for its emerald mines. These gems, some of the world's finest, were highly sought after by emperors and traders. Mining them remains a traditional craft in the region.
36. *The Bamiyan Valley* is in the Bamyan Province in Central Afghanistan. Its capital is Bamiyan. Bamiyan is at an altitude of about 8,366 feet above sea level. The Bamyan Airport is located in the middle of the city. The airport's high-altitude location, combined with its relatively short runway, historically presented landing challenges for pilots.

37. The region is famous for various Bamiyan Buddhas and has a lot of Buddhist influence. These were built by Buddhist monks over a thousand years ago, with construction estimated to have started around the 6th or 7th century CE. They are a *UNESCO World Heritage Site*.
38. In Bamyan, Researchers discovered remnants of oil paintings, behind the famous (now destroyed) Bamyan Statues, dating back to the 7th century CE, making them among the earliest known uses of oil-based artworks in history.
39. Near Bamiyan lies Shahr-e-Zohak, an ancient fortress often called the "Red City" due to its red clay walls. This 6th-century structure was a key defensive site on the Silk Road. Its strategic location allowed it to guard important trade routes against invading forces.
40. Afghanistan is known to be the oldest known source of Lapis Lazuli, a vibrant blue gemstone prized for its intense color and durability. For over 6,000 years, the mines of Afghanistan have yielded this precious stone, which has been highly valued across civilizations.
41. Afghanistan has a lot of tourist potential. Beautiful lakes like the Band-e Amir, Supreme Summits of the Hindu Kush Mountains and River Valleys around the whole country. There are restrictions but if they could be overcome, beauty and serenity lies ahead.

42. Afghanistan has a rich history and has been home to various civilisations such as the Indus Valley Civilisation, Bactria-Margiana Archaeological Complex, Achaemenid Empire, Greco-Bactrian Kingdom, Kushan Empire and the Gandhara Civilisation. Works of These Ancient Civilisations today are Archaeological Wonders. Through these Civilisations, Buddhist, Zoroastrianist, Christian and Islamic ideas spread. Buddhism shapes a major part of Afghan history. Islam came much more recently. Alexander the Great also invaded parts of Afghanistan. The Mongol Empire also had Afghanistan in its territories once.
43. *Mundigak*, near modern-day Kandahar, was an advanced Bronze Age settlement dating back to 3,000 BCE. Archaeologists uncovered multi-storey buildings, intricate pottery, and irrigation systems. It demonstrates Afghanistan's role in the ancient Indus Valley civilization.
44. *The Bactrian Gold*, also known as the Bactrian Treasure, is a stunning collection of ancient gold artifacts discovered in Afghanistan in 1978. The Bactrian Gold is significant not only for its beauty and craftsmanship but also for its historical importance. The treasure provides a unique glimpse into the culture, trade, and traditions of ancient Bactria, which was a major center of civilization in the ancient world.

45. The lost city of *Ai-Khanoum* in Northeastern Afghanistan, is a Greco-Bactrian city located in northern Afghanistan that was uncovered in the 1960s, showing Greek influence with theaters, gymnasiums, and temples.
46. *Nuristan*, once called *Kafiristan* in Northeastern Afghanistan , remained isolated until the 19th century. Its people practiced an animist religion before converting to Islam. Legends claim the valley is home to remnants of Alexander the Great's army, who allegedly settled there.
47. Archeologists have discovered subterranean Buddhist temples near Mes Aynak, dating back to the Kushan Empire. The Mes Aynak site also has one of the world's largest copper deposits, alongside significant Buddhist archaeological remains.
48. Since Afghanistan had various advanced Civilisations such as the Indus Valley Civilisation, Afghanistan is also home to some of the oldest irrigation systems in the world, dating back over 2,000 years. Afghanistan has several underground rivers that supply water to remote areas. The most famous are part of the *karez* system, an ancient irrigation technique still in use today.
49. Soon after Buddhist movements, there was a wave of Persian influence and soon Islam arrived. Gradually Islam became Afghanistan's major religion.

50. Afghanistan was also once a major center of Zoroastrianism, an ancient Persian religion.
51. Grapes have been cultivated in Afghanistan for over 7,000 years, particularly in the region of Kandahar. During Zoroastrianism times, Afghanistan was a huge producer of wine.
52. The Avesta, the sacred text of Zoroastrianism, mentions regions of modern Afghanistan as part of its holy geography. Herat and Balkh are considered significant Zoroastrian centers in ancient times. Fire temples in these areas attest to this legacy.
53. *Balkh*, in northern Afghanistan, is considered one of the world's oldest continuously inhabited cities. Known as Bactra in antiquity, it was a key center for Zoroastrianism and Buddhism. Ancient Balkh, once called Bactra, was a hub of learning and spirituality. Referred to as the *"Mother of Cities,"* much of its grandeur now lies buried under layers of earth. It was a prominent Buddhist center before becoming a key site for early Islam.
54. The Minaret of Jam is a majestic 12th-century minaret located in the remote Ghor Province of Afghanistan. This towering structure is one of the tallest minarets in the world and a testament to the rich cultural heritage of Afghanistan. It is the only other *UNESCO World Heritage Site* in Afghanistan other than the *Bamiyan Valley Remains.*

55. The greatest empires in South-east Asia such as the Ghaznavid Empire, Mughal Empire, Durrani Empire were formed with origins in Afghanistan. They were highly dominant and were feared by their neighbours. Their supremacy ended during the colonial times, where they were taken over by Russian and British empires.
56. Afghanistan gained its full independence from British influence in ***1919*** following the Third Anglo-Afghan War. The country had been involved in earlier conflicts with Britain, beginning with the First Anglo-Afghan War in 1839, but it was never fully colonized.
57. Afghanistan transitioned from a monarchy to a republic in 1973, 54 years after its Full Independence.
58. Soviet forces once tried to invade Afghanistan to extend their territory and to support the Communist Government in Afghanistan. This war had a profound impact on the region, leading to a civil war and heavy militarisation and ultimately contributed to the collapse of the Soviet Union.
59. Afghan Culture is very diverse due to many ethnicities that live here and also due to the rich history of many cultures. There are many traditions and languages owing to the same reason.
60. Traditional music and dance forms are an integral part of Afghan culture. Traditional music is performed

with various instruments such as the rubab, tabla and dutar.

61. *Herat* has a unique musical tradition blending Persian, Indian, and Central Asian styles. Historical records suggest that Afghan musicians were once prominent in the courts of emperors like Akbar of the Mughal Empire. Instruments like the rubab and tabla trace some roots to this region.
62. Due to Islamic past and gradual majority of the Sufi sect, Sufism and Sufi values have a strong presence in Afghan society.
63. *Pashtunwali* is a traditional Pashtun code of honour, and hospitality. Afghans are famous around the world due to their warm hospitality and generosity towards guests.
64. Just like music, Poetry and Literature are also an integral part of Afghan culture and traditions. Renowned poets like Rumi, made this fact famous to the world.
65. Afghani Carpets for their intricate designs and craftsmanship are renowned all over the world. Just like Persian carpets, their quality is like no other, and to compare those with something else is useless.
66. Afghani cuisine is very unique, having influences from Central Asia, Middle East and India. The cuisine is rice centric, meat focused, has Spice usage and Usage of Fresh Produce and Breads.

Some dishes are: Afghani Kebabs, Kabuli Pulao, Mantu, Ashak, Bolani, Borani Banjan, Shor Nakhod and Haft Mewa.

67. Traditional Dresses vary from regions to ethnicities. Striking Colours of Dresses and Intricate Embroidery are stuff that stands out.
68. Festivals such as Navrouz and Eid are followed throughout Afghanistan.
69. Afghanistan has a rich and long-standing tradition of miniature painting, an art form renowned for its intricate detail, vibrant colors, and meticulous craftsmanship. These small-scale paintings often depict royal courts, battles, literary tales, and religious stories, blending realism with highly stylized patterns. Afghan miniature painting was deeply influenced by Persian, Timurid, and Mughal artistic traditions, reflecting Afghanistan's position as a cultural crossroads along the Silk Road.
70. Just after Soviet interests in Afghanistan died, a Conservative Islamist group named Taliban was formed. The Taliban group helped the Al-Qaeda terrorist group led by Osama bin Laden, launch the infamous 9/11 attacks on the World Trade Centre resulting in about 3000 deaths. This led to the US Invading Afghanistan in 2001 and the Taliban regime was ousted from power. Taliban insurgency continued despite International efforts. In 2021, US forces

withdrew themselves and the Taliban regime took control of the Government again.

71. The Afghan government is an Islamic totalitarian government with a Presidential System.

72. Before the Taliban's initial takeover of the Afghan Government, Afghanistan did not have a written national anthem, only instrumental music.

73. Afghanistan has complex relations with the international community but relies heavily on international aid. The International community provided significant aid for reconstruction and development.

74. The country faces various challenges which are political and social. The country is politically unstable and sectors are filled with corruption. The economy faces various challenges like poverty, limited education, inadequate health care, child labour, displacement due to violence and violation of human rights like freedom of speech and expression.

75. The Absolute Barring Education of Girls in Afghanistan is a myth. Most of us know that girls in Afghanistan are not allowed to go to school or work. But that's not actually true.
Girls are allowed to go to school till the age of 12 and from there, if the girl desires to further her education, it must be done either by homeschooling or online classes. They are allowed to go to certain (yet limited)

fields of study and university, mostly in the educational or medical sector, as there is a demand for female doctors since male doctors are not allowed to perform certain procedures on women. Women are allowed to work in certain fields as well. Most of them include services that cater to women such as female security guards and female teachers, female tailors and so on. Occasionally they could even be found in an office or a ticket counter.

76. Zablon Simintov is known to be *"The Last Jew living in the whole of Afghanistan"*. He lived in Kabul. He used to own a restaurant and maintained the only last synagogue in Afghanistan. He evacuated to Israel in 2021 after the Taliban took control of the nation.

77. Even though Afghanistan has a controversial reputation, its behavior on the international stage is often erratic, as mentioned earlier. Afghanistan considers Türkiye as their best friend. They cooperated with each other peacefully for over centuries.

    There's also an Afghani saying: "No Afghani was ever killed by a Türkish bullet and no Afghani trained by a Türk, ever betrayed his country."

78. In Afghanistan, birds are preferred to be the number one house pet. Bird markets are found all over the country. In Afghan culture, birds are considered a symbol of beauty, freedom, and good luck. Many

Afghans keep birds as pets, particularly songbirds like nightingales, partridges, and sparrows. These birds are prized for their beautiful songs and are often kept in decorative cages.

79. "Non Wayi Sayar" or "mobile bakeries" could be seen all over the roadside. These are little glass kiosks that sell bread on the street.
80. All taxis in Afghanistan by law, must be a shade of light blue. Taxi fares are also really cheap.
81. Since many cars are illegally imported in Afghanistan, cars with curious licence plates from all over the world could be seen which are definitely not from Afghanistan (unfortunately).
82. Most Produce and Street Food in Afghanistan are Wrapped up in Korean Newspapers. Afghanistan has a deal with South Korea where South Korea sells it to Afghanistan for cheaper than the price of conventional packaging material.

    South Korea has also been donating a lot of money as international aid. From 2022 to 2024, South Korea had donated $1 million USD as general aid, and $43 million USD as help in securing basic rights and improving women's rights in Afghanistan. Trade also has been flourishing between these countries in the years mentioned. Major things traded in the mentioned years were beverages, electrical equipment, pharmaceutical products, salt, apparel and footwear.

83. The national sport of Afghanistan is *Buzkashi*. The sport has few rules and is considered as one of the wildest and dangerous games on the entire planet. Basically, it originated with the Mongols but then it was adopted and revised by the Afghans. It is a game played on horses in which the players have to grab a Goat carcass and drop it off at a designated chalked off circle area.
84. *Falconry*, the art of hunting with trained birds of prey, has been practiced in Afghanistan for centuries and holds deep cultural significance, especially among the Pashtun and nomadic communities. It blends tradition, skill, and a deep connection to nature.
85. Afghanistan also has their own Bruce Lee impersonator, martial arts expert and enthusiast. *Abbas Alizada* has been following his dream of being a professional Bruce Lee impersonator and Martial Artist.
86. In Afghanistan, Fridays are a holiday and most businesses, government offices, schools and universities are closed. Traditional events or social events like a wedding are arranged usually on Fridays.
87. Afghanistan's rugged terrain and mountainous landscape have necessitated the construction of tunnels to facilitate transportation, commerce, and communication. These tunnels have played a crucial role in the country's history, economy, and military strategies. There are tunnels for railway, roads and the

military.
Notable tunnels are the Salang Tunnel, the Hajigak Tunnel and the Tunel-e-Hairatan tunnel.
The *Salang Tunnel* is a 2.6 km tunnel connecting Kabul to northern Afghanistan, reducing travel time and improving safety.
The *Hajigak Tunnel* is a 2.2 km tunnel on the Kabul-Bamiyan highway, improving access to central Afghanistan.
The *Tunel-e-Hairatan* tunnel is a tunnel on the Afghanistan-Uzbekistan border, facilitating international trade and commerce.

88. Afghanistan contains roads falling under the All Weather Roads System. All-weather roads enable uninterrupted transportation throughout the year, regardless of weather conditions. Enhanced road surfaces and design features reduce the risk of accidents and improve overall road safety. All-weather roads facilitate faster and more efficient transportation of goods and people, stimulating economic growth and development.
Notable All Weather Roads in Afghanistan are the Kabul-Jalalabad Road, Kandahar-Herat Highway and the Ring Road.
The Kabul-Jalalabad Road is a 153 km highway linking Kabul to Jalalabad making it a major trade route with Pakistan.

The Kandahar-Herat Highway is a 600 km road connecting Kandahar to Herat, improving access to western Afghanistan.

The Ring Road is a 2,200 km highway encircling the country, enhancing connectivity between provinces and facilitating regional trade.

89. The city of Herat is called the *Marble City* because of its abundant high-quality marble deposits, which have been used in construction and art for centuries.

The city is home to the Chesht-i-Sharif marble deposits, which are known for their high-quality marble, and a growing number of marble-cutting factories have been established there, creating thousands of jobs.

This industry has helped boost the local economy, and Herat marble has even been donated to other countries for large construction projects, such as the Imam Bukhari complex in Uzbekistan.

90. The tradition of flying and battling kites, popularized by Khaled Hosseini's *The Kite Runner*, has ancient roots in Afghan culture. It remains a symbol of joy and freedom, despite bans during the Taliban's first regime.

91. The Koh-e Baba Mountains (in one of the many mountain ranges in Central Afghanistan mentioned before) is home to wild tulips and other endemic plants, some of which are not found anywhere else in the world. Some of the flowers found in this region include Wild Tulips, Iris, Anemones, Poppy Flowers, Edelweiss, Blue

Gentians, Buttercups, Wild Primroses, Alpine Forget-me-nots, Wild Marigolds, Mountain Daisies and Crocuses.

92. In Afghanistan's deserts, rare crocus flowers bloom briefly after seasonal rains. These blooms are not only beautiful but also a vital source of nectar for local bees. They symbolise resilience in harsh environments.

93. Queen Kubaba of Sumer, thought to be of Afghan origin, is one of the earliest recorded female rulers in history.

94. Afghanistan is home to the *Marco Polo sheep*, known for their massive, spiraling horns and high-altitude habitats.

95. In remote parts of the Pamir Mountains, there grow shrubs known locally as "Marco Polo bushes." These resilient plants survive extreme conditions and are named after the explorer who documented them in his travels.

96. The eastern region of Afghanistan has traditional vertical-axis windmills dating back over 1,000 years. These unique windmills were used to grind grain and are some of the earliest examples of wind energy technology. Their vertical design is perfectly suited to the region's harsh winds.

97. The Dasht-e-Nawar plain in Ghazni province hosts seasonal salt lakes surrounded by migratory bird habitats. Flamingos are known to nest here, an unusual

sight for this landlocked region. The area has been a vital salt production site for centuries.

98. Afghanistan was once a major producer of *attar* (natural perfume) made from rose petals and other flowers. Herat and Kandahar were centers of this fragrant industry. The perfumes were exported along the Silk Road to Persia, India, and beyond
99. The Spin Ghar mountains are home to ancient petroglyphs carved into rocks by early settlers. These carvings depict hunting scenes, animals, and religious symbols. They provide a window into prehistoric life in the region.
100. In the eastern province of Laghman, locals speak of "Dragon Trees" that bleed red sap when cut. These rare trees, believed to have mystical properties, are a source of resin used in traditional medicine. They are linked to ancient myths about dragons that once roamed the mountains.
101. In Conclusion, The list of natural wonders that look mythical, hidden treasures that get found by explorers, cultural diversity and ethnicities of different varieties would never end. Putting aside all the modern day controversies, Afghanistan is actually a very beautiful country with a very rich and vibrant history, cultures and traditions, yet often hidden cultural and historical past that very often goes overlooked.

Image References for the Facts

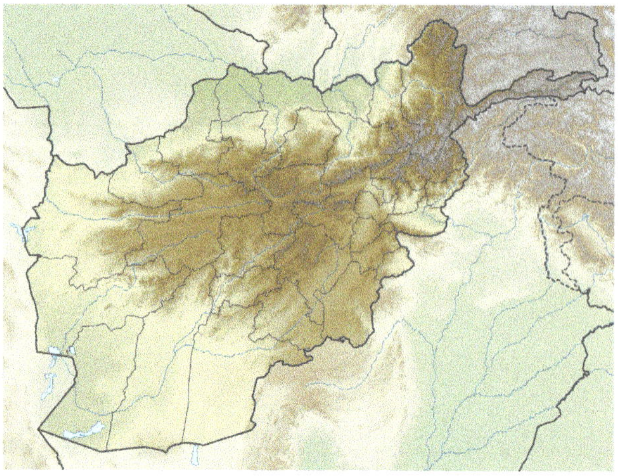

Physical Map of Afghanistan

Map of Afghanistan (with neighbours)

Hindu Kush Mountains

Hindu Kush Mountains Black Ice Glaciers

Snow Leopards

Afghani Saffron

Afghani Pistachio Forests

Opium poppy

Kabul

Kabul City Walls

Mandavi Bazaar

The Paghman Gardens

Afghan Afghani

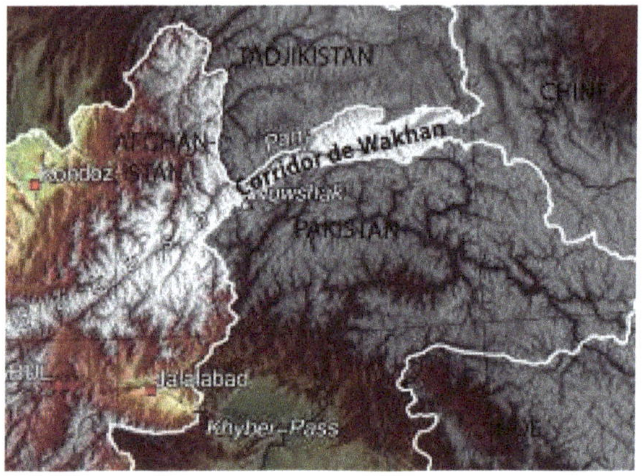

The Wakhan Corridor

Lake Chaqmaqtin

Tange Gharu Canyon

Amu Darya River

Helmand River

Lashkar Gah

Lashkari Bazaar

Kabul River

Band-e Amir

Panjshir Valley

Bamiyan Valley

Shahr-e-Zohak

Lapis Lazuli

Mundigak

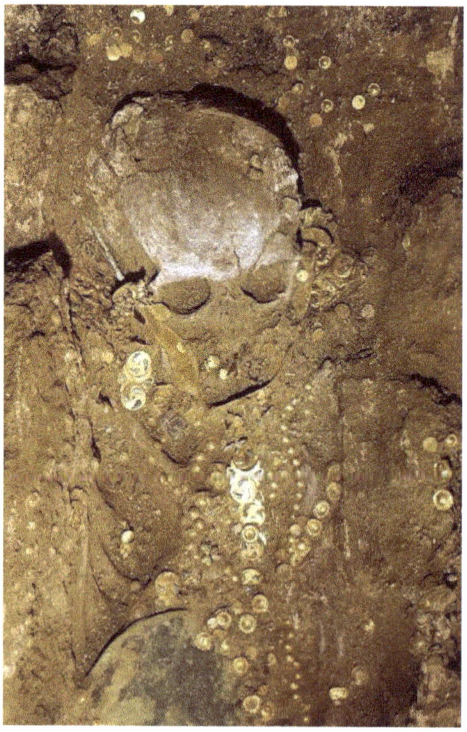

The Bactrian Gold

Ai-Khanoum

Kafiristan

Mes Aynak

Mes Aynak underground Buddhist Temples

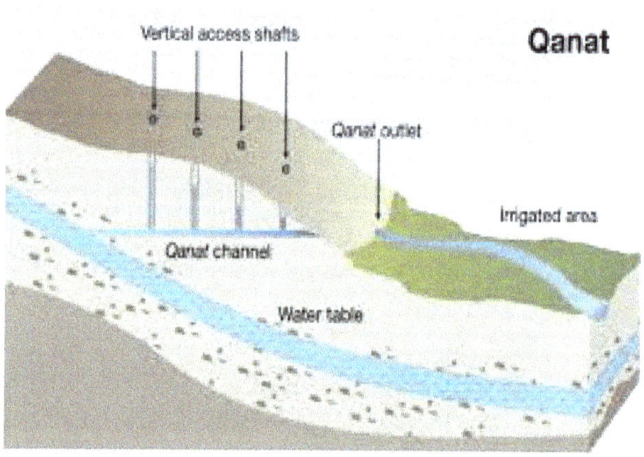

Karez System

Silk Route

Minaret of Jam

Afghani people

Traditional Afghan Music

Rumi

Afghani Carpets

Afghani Kebabs

Kabuli Pulao

Mantu

Ashak

Bolani

Borani Banjan

Shor Nakhod

Haft Mewa

Traditional Dresses

Miniature Art

Taliban

Zablon Simintov

Afghani Bird Market

Non Wayi Sayar

Light Blue Afghani Taxis

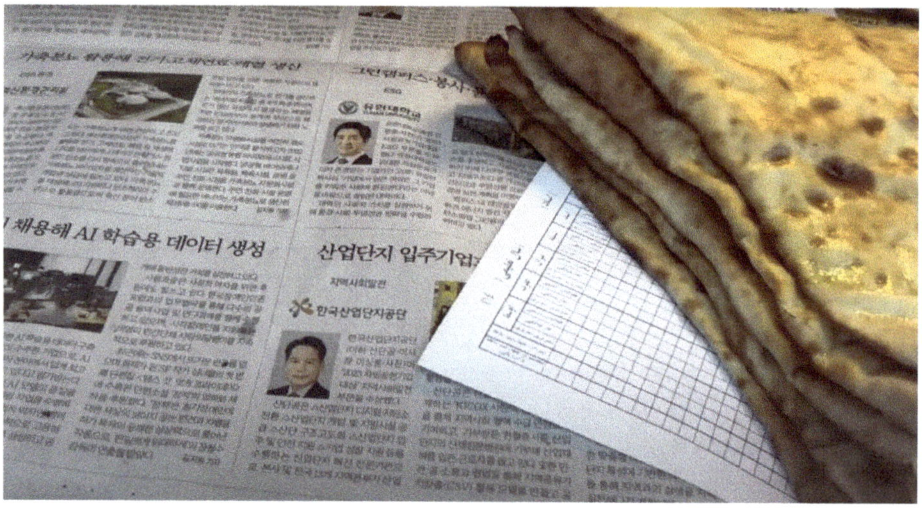

Afghan Markets using Korean Newspapers

Buzkashi

Afghan Falconry

Abbas Alizada

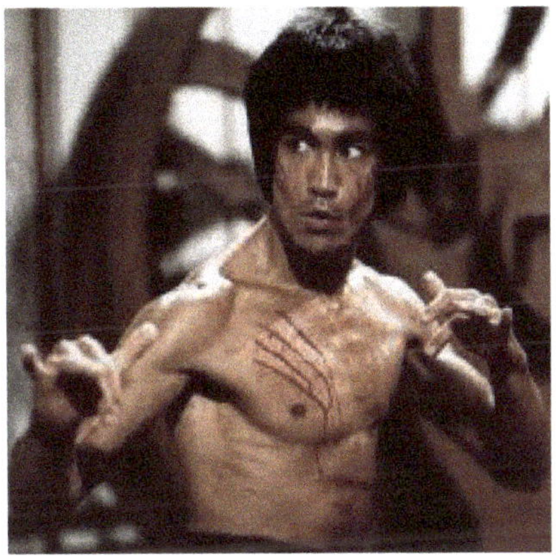

Bruce Lee

Afghani Tunnel System

Kabul-Jalalabad Road (All Weather Road)

Herat: The Marble City

Khaled Hosseini

Afghan Kites

Balkh

Koh-e Baba Mountains

Crocus Flowers in Afghani Deserts

Queen Kubaba of Sumer

Marco Polo Sheep

Traditional Afghan windmills

Salt lakes in Dasht-e-Nawar

Afghani natural perfumes

Spin Ghar Mountains

Afghani Dragon Trees

A Huge Thank You To Those Who Provided the Images. Unfortunately I haven't listed my sources .Apologies for that. Will Do That Next Time.

For further information: author.ritesh@gmail.com

www.ingramcontent.com/pod-product-compliance
Ingram Content Group UK Ltd.
Pitfield, Milton Keynes, MK11 3LW, UK
UKHW061540190726
13845UKWH00031B/1129

9 789356 028487